READING POWER

19th Century American Inventors

The Inventions of

Eli Whitney

The Cotton Gin

Holly Cefrey

The Rosen Publishing Group's
PowerKids Press™
New York

Published in 2003 by The Rosen Publishing Group, Inc.
29 East 21st Street, New York, NY 10010

First Edition

Book Design: Daniel Hosek

Photo Credits: Cover, pp. 6–7, 8–9, 10–11, 20, 21 © North Wind Picture Archives; pp. 4, 13 (foreground) © Culver Pictures; p. 5 © Corbis; p. 11 (inset) © PhotoDisc; pp. 13 (background), 15, 16–17, 18 Library of Congress, Division of Prints and Photographs; p. 14 © Milepost 92 1/2/Corbis; p. 19 © Minnesota Historical Society/Corbis

Library of Congress Cataloging-in-Publication Data

Cefrey, Holly.
The inventions of Eli Whitney : the cotton gin / Holly Cefrey.
    p. cm. — (19th century American inventors)
Summary: Provides a biographical sketch of Eli Whitney and a description of his most famous invention, the cotton gin, which made the harvesting of cotton easier.
ISBN 0-8239-6443-4 (library binding)
1. Whitney, Eli, 1765-1825—Juvenile literature. 2. Inventors—United States—Biography—Juvenile literature. 3. Cotton gins and ginning—Juvenile literature. [1. Whitney, Eli, 1765-1825. 2. Inventors. 3. Cotton gins and ginning.] I. Title. II. Series.
TS1570.W4 C44 2003
609.2—dc21

2002000176

Contents

Young Eli Whitney

Eli Whitney was born in Westborough, Massachusetts, on December 8, 1765. His parents were Eli and Elizabeth Whitney. He was one of four children. Whitney and his family lived on a farm.

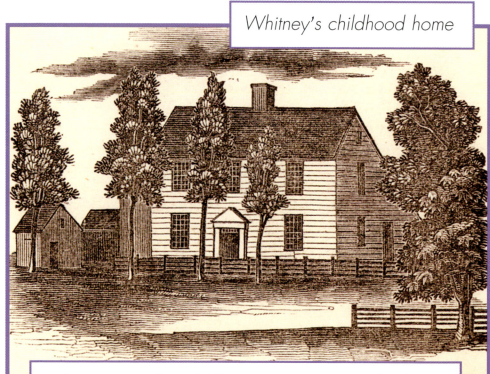

Whitney's childhood home

As a young boy, Whitney was interested in how things worked. He also liked to make things.

Eli Whitney

The Fact Box

As a teenager during the Revolutionary War, Whitney started a small business. He made and sold nails.

College Days

When Whitney was in his early twenties, he decided he wanted a college education. He went to Yale College in New Haven, Connecticut, and graduated in 1792. After college, Whitney was offered a job as a teacher in South Carolina.

Yale College was renamed Yale University in 1887.

On his way to South Carolina, Whitney met Catherine Greene. Greene owned a cotton plantation in Georgia. When his teaching job fell through, Greene let Whitney live on her plantation until he found a job. In return, Whitney fixed and improved the tools at the plantation.

Southern states, such as South Carolina and Georgia, had many plantations. Cotton and tobacco were two main crops grown on plantations.

The Cotton Gin

In 1793, Greene asked Whitney to try to make a machine to take the seeds out of picked cotton. Whitney invented a machine that could clean cotton faster than a person could. He called his invention the cotton gin.

Cotton plant

Whitney saw how hard it was for a person to remove seeds from cotton by hand. It took an entire day to clean one pound of cotton by hand.

Whitney was given a patent for his invention. He was the only one who could make and sell cotton gins. Whitney started a business to make and sell cotton gins. Many farmers wanted cotton gins. However, Whitney could not make them fast enough to fill the orders he got.

The Fact Box

Gin is short for engine.

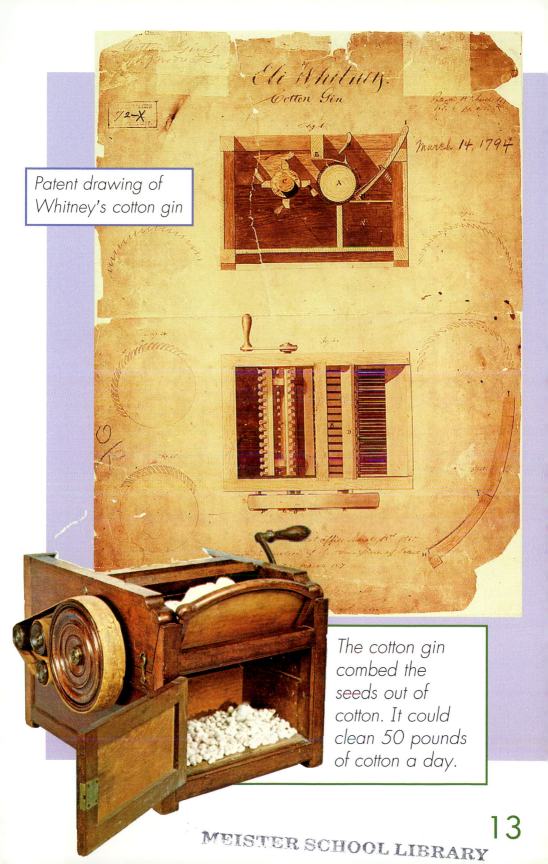

Patent drawing of Whitney's cotton gin

The cotton gin combed the seeds out of cotton. It could clean 50 pounds of cotton a day.

13

Other people began making copies of Whitney's invention. They did not want to wait a long time for Whitney to make the machines. Whitney went to court to stop them. It took Whitney about ten years to stop others from making cotton gins like his. He lost a lot of money trying to keep the rights to his invention.

What Cotton Can Make

One bale, or bundle, of cotton weighs about 500 pounds.

One bale of cotton can make:

313,600 $100 bills,

or

1,217 men's T-shirts,

or

4,321 women's socks.

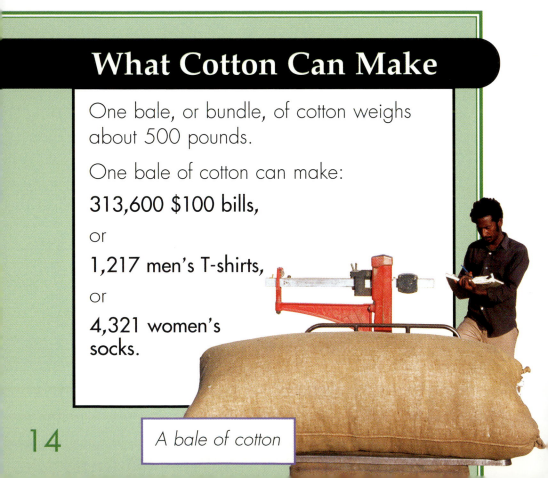

14

A bale of cotton

Whitney wrote to the U.S. government asking to let him keep the rights to his cotton gin.

"An invention can be so valuable as to be worthless to the inventor."
—Eli Whitney, talking about his cotton gin patent troubles

New Ways to Make Things

Whitney moved back to New Haven, Connecticut, where he continued to work on other ideas. He invented a system of using machines in a new way. Using Whitney's system of mass production, workers could make a lot of the same things quickly.

In 1798, Whitney agreed to use mass production to make 10,000 muskets for the U.S. government.

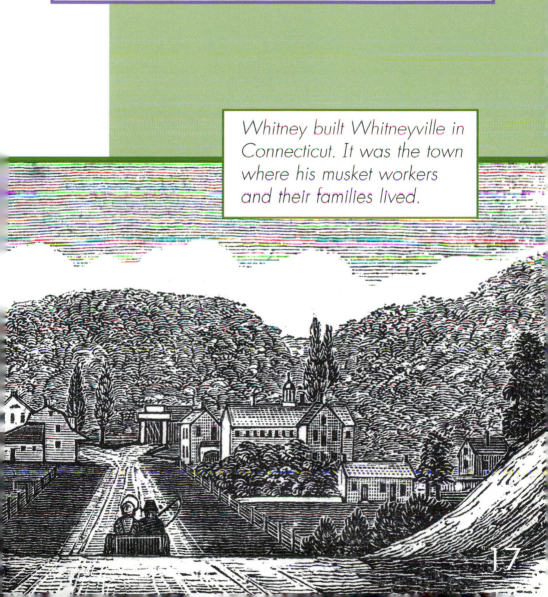

Whitney built Whitneyville in Connecticut. It was the town where his musket workers and their families lived.

Whitney made machines to make each part of a musket. Workers then put the different parts together to make a finished musket. The parts of each musket were interchangeable.

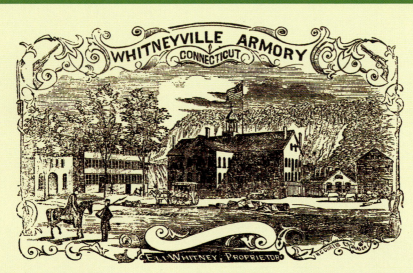

WHITNEYVILLE ARMORY
CONNECTICUT

Eli Whitney, Proprietor

WHITNEY'S IMPROVED FIRE-ARMS.

Whitney's business in Connecticut made thousands of muskets for the U.S. government.

Many different kinds of factories started to use mass production as a way to make goods quickly. These factory workers, from 1935, used mass production to build cars. A form of Whitney's mass production is still used today.

What Whitney Gave the World

Eli Whitney died on January 8, 1825. Whitney gave the world an invention that improved the way cotton was gathered and cleaned. He also found a way for factories to make goods faster. Eli Whitney's inventions are still used today.

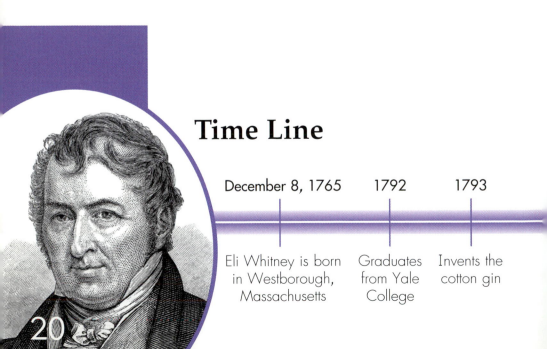

Time Line

December 8, 1765	1792	1793
Eli Whitney is born in Westborough, Massachusetts	Graduates from Yale College	Invents the cotton gin

A form of Whitney's cotton gin is used today on many of the 35,000 cotton farms in the United States.

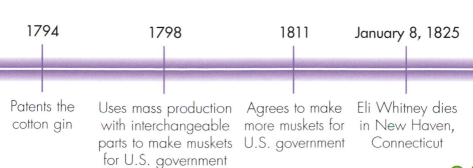

1794	1798	1811	January 8, 1825
Patents the cotton gin	Uses mass production with interchangeable parts to make muskets for U.S. government	Agrees to make more muskets for U.S. government	Eli Whitney dies in New Haven, Connecticut

Glossary

college (**kahl**-ihj) a school where people can study after high school

cotton gin (**kaht**-uhn **jihn**) a machine that takes the seeds out of cotton

factories (**fak**-tuhr-eez) places where things are made using machines

graduated (**graj**-oo-ayt-uhd) having finished school

interchangeable (ihn-tuhr-**chayn**-juh-buhl) able to be put or used in place of each other

invention (ihn-**vehn**-shuhn) something new that someone thinks of or makes

mass production (**mas** pruh-**duhk**-shuhn) a way of making a lot of the same things quickly in a factory

musket (**muhs**-kiht) a gun with a long barrel that was used from the 16th to the mid-19th century

patent (**pat**-uhnt) a legal paper that gives an inventor the rights to make or sell his or her invention

plantation (plan-**tay**-shuhn) a large farm where crops, such as cotton or tobacco, are grown

university (yoo-nuh-**vehr**-suh-tee) a school where people go after high school

Resources

Books

Eli Whitney: Great Inventor
by Jean Lee Latham
Chelsea House Publishers (1991)

From Plant to Blue Jeans: A Photo Essay
by Arthur John L'Hommedieu
Children's Press (1998)

Web Sites

Due to the changing nature of Internet links, PowerKids Press has developed an on-line list of Web sites related to the subjects of this book. This site is updated regularly. Please use this link to access the list:

http://www.powerkidslinks.com/ncai/iew/

Index

C
college, 7, 20

cotton, 9–11, 13–14, 20

cotton gin, 10, 12–15, 20–21

F
factories, 19–20

G
Greene, Catherine, 8, 10

I
invention, 10, 12, 14–15, 20

M
mass production, 16–17, 19, 21

musket, 17–18, 21

P
patent, 12–13, 15, 21

plantation, 8–9

Word Count: 414

Note to Librarians, Teachers, and Parents

If reading is a challenge, Reading Power is a solution! Reading Power is perfect for readers who want high-interest subject matter at an accessible reading level. These fact-filled, photo-illustrated books are designed for readers who want straightforward vocabulary, engaging topics, and a manageable reading experience. With clear picture/text correspondence, leveled Reading Power books put the reader in charge. Now readers have the power to get the information they want and the skills they need in a user-friendly format.